Dedication

To all those who ever struggled with learning a
foreign language and to Wolfgang Karfunkel

Also by Yatir Nitzany

Conversational Spanish Quick and Easy

....

Conversational Italian Quick and Easy

....

Conversational French Quick and Easy

....

Conversational Portuguese Quick and Easy

....

Conversational Russian Quick and Easy

....

Conversational Polish Quick and Easy

....

Conversational Hebrew Quick and Easy

....

Conversational Yiddish Quick and Easy

....

Conversational Arabic Quick and Easy
Classical Arabic

....

Conversational Arabic Quick and Easy
Lebanese Dialect

....

Conversational Arabic Quick and Easy
Palestinian Dialect

....

Conversational Arabic Quick and Easy
Egyptian Dialect

....

Conversational Arabic Quick and Easy
Jordanian Dialect

....

Conversational Arabic Quick and Easy
Emirati Dialect

....

Conversational Arabic Quick and Easy
Syrian Arabic

Conversational Dutch Quick and Easy

YATIR NITZANY

Printed in the United States of America

Foreword

About Myself

For many years I struggled to learn Spanish, and I still knew no more than about twenty words. Consequently, I was extremely frustrated. One day I stumbled upon this method as I was playing around with word combinations. Suddenly, I came to the realization that every language has a certain core group of words that are most commonly used and, simply by learning them, one could gain the ability to engage in quick and easy conversational Spanish.

I discovered which words those were, and I narrowed them down to three hundred and fifty that, once memorized, one could connect and create one's own sentences. The variations were and are *infinite*! By using this incredibly simple technique, I could converse at a proficient level and speak Spanish. Within a week, I astonished my Spanish-speaking friends with my newfound ability. The next semester I registered at my university for a Spanish language course, and I applied the same principles I had learned in that class (grammar, additional vocabulary, future and past tense, etc.) to those three hundred and fifty words I already had memorized, and immediately I felt as if I had grown wings and learned how to fly.

At the end of the semester, we took a class trip to San José, Costa Rica. I was like a fish in water, while the rest of my classmates were floundering and still struggling to converse. Throughout the following months, I again applied the same principle to other languages—French, Portuguese, Italian, and Arabic, all of which I now speak proficiently, thanks to this very simple technique.

This method is by far the fastest way to master quick and easy conversational language skills. There is no other technique that compares to my concept. It is effective, it worked for me, and it will work for you. Be consistent with my program, and you too will succeed the way I and many, many others have.

Contents

INTRODUCTION TO
THE PROGRAM

People often dream about learning a foreign language, but usually they never do it. Some feel that they just won't be able to do it while others believe that they don't have the time. Whatever your reason is, it's time to set that aside. With my new method, you will have enough time, and you will not fail. You will actually learn how to speak the fundamentals of the language—fluently in as little as a few days. Of course, you won't speak perfect Dutch at first, but you will certainly gain significant proficiency. For example, if you travel to the Netherlands, you will almost effortlessly be able engage in basic conversational communication with the locals in the present tense and you will no longer be intimidated by culture shock. It's time to relax. Learning a language is a valuable skill that connects people of multiple cultures around the world —and you now have the tools to join them.

How does my method work? I have taken twenty-seven of the most commonly used languages in the world and distilled from them the three hundred and fifty most frequently used words in any language. This process took three years of observation and research, and during that time, I determined which words I felt were most important for this method of basic conversational communication. In that time, I chose these words in such a way that they were structurally interrelated and that, when combined, form sentences. Thus, once you succeed in memorizing these words, you will be able to combine these words and form your own sentences. The words are spread over twenty pages. In fact, there are just nine basic words that will effectively build bridges, enabling you to speak in an understandable manner (please see Building Bridges. The words will also combine easily in sentences, for example, enabling you to ask simple questions, make basic statements, and obtain a rudimentary understanding of others' communications. I have also created Memorization-Made-Easy Techniques for this program in order to help with the memorization of the vocabulary. Please see Reading and Pronunciation in order to gain proficiency in the reading and pronunciation of the Dutch language prior to starting this program.

My book is mainly intended for basic present tense vocal communication, meaning anyone can easily use it to "get by" linguistically while visiting a foreign country without learning the entire language. With practice, you will be 100 percent understandable to native speakers, which is your aim. One disclaimer: this is not a grammar book, though it does address minute and essential grammar rules (please keep your eyes peeled for grammar footnotes at the bottom of each and every page of the program). Therefore, understanding complex sentences with obscure words in Dutch is beyond the scope of this book.

People who have tried this method have been successful, and by the time you finish this book, you will understand and be understood in basic conversational Dutch. This is the best basis to learn not only the Dutch language but any language. This is an entirely revolutionary, no-fail concept, and your ability to combine the pieces of the "language puzzle" together will come with great ease, especially if you use this program prior to beginning a Dutch class.

This is the best program that was ever designed to teach the reader how to become conversational. Other conversational programs will only teach you phrases. But this is the only program that will teach you how to create your own sentences for the purpose of becoming conversational.

THE DUTCH LANGUAGE

Dutch is not only the national language of the Netherlands but is also a national language of Belgium, and Suriname and the Dutch Antilles in South America. In Belgium, it's the official language of Flanders, the Northern region of the country, and is also spoken in Brussels by a minority. In Suriname and the Dutch Antilles, Dutch is still an official language but alongside several other languages.

Worldwide, there are over 23 million native speakers of Dutch. It is a popular second language in Germany and the north of France, and it's a growing language in Eastern Europe.

Dutch and English are languages that come from the same old Germanic root and Dutch is the third most popular Germanic language after English and German. Dutch vocabulary is mostly Germanic and incorporates more loan words from Romance languages than German but fewer than English. In both Belgium and the Netherlands, the native official name for Dutch is Nederlands, and its dialects have their own names, e.g. Hollands ("Hollandic"), West-Vlaams ("West Flemish"), and Brabants ("Brabantian").

The word Dutch was derived from the Old Germanic word theudisk, one of the first names ever used for the non-Romance languages of Western Europe. It literarily means "the language of the common people," that is, the native Germanic language. The term was used in opposition to Latin, which was the non-native language of writing and of the Catholic Church.

Spoken in: The Netherlands, Belgium, Suriname, & Dutch Antilles

MEMORIZATION MADE EASY

There is no doubt the three hundred and fifty words in my program are the required essentials in order to engage in quick and easy basic conversation in any foreign language. However, some people may experience difficulty in the memorization. For this reason, I created Memorization Made Easy. This memorization technique will make this program so simple and fun that it's unbelievable! I have spread the words over the following twenty pages. Each page contains a vocabulary table of ten to fifteen words. Below every vocabulary box, sentences are composed from the words on the page that you have just studied. This aids greatly in memorization. Once you succeed in memorizing the first page, then proceed to the second page. Upon completion of the second page, go back to the first and review. Then proceed to the third page. After memorizing the third, go back to the first and second and repeat. And so on. As you continue, begin to combine words and create your own sentences in your head. Every time you proceed to the following page, you will notice words from the previous pages will be present in those simple sentences as well, because repetition is one of the most crucial aspects in learning any foreign language. Upon completion of your twenty pages, congratulations, you have absorbed the required words and gained a basic, quick-and-easy proficiency and you should now be able to create your own sentences and say anything you wish in Dutch. This is a crash course in conversational Dutch, and it works!

DUTCH PRONUNCIATION

Vowels can be pronounced long or short, depending on whether they are followed by no, one, or two consonants. Diphthongs existing of two of the same vowels are pronounced in the same way as if a single one would be followed by no or one consonant.

a (short) – "ah" as in father
a (long) and *aa* – "ah" as in father but longer
e (short) – "eh" as in men
e (long) and *ee* – as the "a" in maze
i – as the "i" in bit
o (short) – "oh" as in of
o (long) and *oo* – "oh" as in boat
u (short) – "uh" as in buzz
u (long) and *uu* – "ew," but pronouncing the "e" a bit longer and the "w" a bit shorter. This sound is not found in English.

Diphthongs
eu – This sound is not found in English, but is pronounced as 'eux' in the French word 'deux'
oe – "ooh" as in pool
ui – combination of a and *uu*
au/ou – as in house
ei/ij – as the "igh" in light and high
j – like the "y" in you
ch/g – a hard sound not found in English. It's a bit like the "J" in the Spanish name Juan.
The best way to describe *ch* or *kh* is to say "ka" or "ha" while at the same time putting your tongue at the back of your throat and blowing air. It's pronounced similarly to the sound that you make while clearing your throat of phlegm. *Please remember this whenever you come across any word containing a *ch* in this program.

NOTE TO THE READER

The purpose of this book is merely to enable you to communicate in Dutch. In the program itself (pages 16-40) you may notice that the composition of some of those sentences might sound rather clumsy. This is intentional. These sentences were formulated in a specific way to serve two purposes: to facilitate the easy memorization of the vocabulary and to teach you how to combine the words in order to form your own sentences for quick and easy communication, rather than making complete literal sense in the English language. So keep in mind that this is not a phrase book!

As the title suggests, the sole purpose of this program is for conversational use only. It is based on the mirror translation technique. These sentences, as well as the translations are not incorrect, just a little clumsy. Latin languages, Semitic languages, and Anglo-Germanic languages, as well as a few others, are compatible with the mirror translation technique.

Many users say that this method surpasses any other known language learning technique that is currently out there on the market. Just stick with the program and you will achieve wonders!

Again, I wish to stress this program is by no means, shape, or form a phrase book! The sole purpose of this book is to give you a fundamental platform to enable you to connect certain words to become conversational. Please also read the "Introduction" and the "About Me" section prior to commencing the program.

In order to succeed with my method, please start on the very first page of the program and fully master one page at a time prior to proceeding to the next. Otherwise, you will overwhelm yourself and fail. Please do not skip pages, nor start from the middle of the book.

It is a myth that certain people are born with the talent to learn a language, and this book disproves that myth. With this method, anyone can learn a foreign language as long as he or she follows these explicit directions:

* Memorize the vocabulary on each page

* Follow that memorization by using a notecard to cover the words you have just memorized and test yourself.

* Then read the sentences following that are created from the vocabulary bank that you just mastered.

* Once fully memorized, give yourself the green light to proceed to the next page.

Again, if you proceed to the following page without mastering the previous, you are guaranteed to gain nothing from this book. If you follow the prescribed steps, you will realize just how effective and simplistic this method is.

THE PROGRAM

Let's Begin! "Vocabulary"
(Memorize the Vocabulary)

I | I am	Ik | Ik ben
With you	Met jou / (Plural) met jullie
With him / with her	Met hem / met haar
With us	Met ons
For you	Voor jou / (Plural) voor jullie
Without him	Zonder hem
Without them	Zonder hen
Always	Altijd
Was	Was
This	Dit
Is	Is
Sometimes	Soms
Today	Vandaag
Are you / you are	Ben je, Zijn jullie
Better	Beter
He / he is	Hij / hij is
She / she is	Zij / zij is
From	Von
You	Jij, je, jou / **plural** - Jullie

Sentences from the vocabulary (now you can speak the sentences and connect the words)

This is for you
Dit is voor jou (Pl.) jullie
I am from the Netherlands
Ik kom uit Nederland
Are you from Amsterdam?
Kom je uit Amsterdam?
I am with you
Ik ben met jou, (pl.) jullie

Sometimes you are with us at the mall
Soms ben je met ons in het winkelcentrum
I am always with her
Ik ben altijd met haar
Are you without them today?
Ben je/ Zijn jullie zonder hen vandaag?
Sometimes I am with him
Soms ben ik met hem

*"I am from ..." or "are you from" can only be translated as "I come from..." The verb "to be" cannot be used in this sentence.

*In Dutch, in the event that a sentence begins with an adverb, the subject and verb change positions in the sentence.

16

I was	Ik was
To be	Zijn
The	De, het
Same	Zelfde
Good	Goed
Here	Hier
It's	Het is
And	En
Between	Tussen
Now	Nu
Later / After	Later / Na
If	Als
Yes	Ja
Then	Dan
Tomorrow	Morgen
OK	Oké
Also / too / as well	Ook

Between now and later
Tussen nu en later
If it's later, then it is better tomorrow
Als het later is, dan is het beter morgen
This is also good
Dit is ook goed
It is the same
Het is hetzelfde
Yes, you are very good
Ja, je bent erg goed
I was here with them
Ik was hier met hen
The same day
Dezelfde dag

*In the Dutch language the masculine form of the article "the" is *de*, the feminine form is also *de*, and the neuter form is *het*. It's sometimes hard to decipher whether a noun is masculine or feminine in the Dutch language, so most people who study this language memorize the article as they go along.
*In the Dutch language in order to indicate "same" we use *zelfde*, however *hetzelfde*, *dezelfde*, and *gelijk* may be used to signify this case as well.

Maybe	Misschien
You	Jij, je, jou
Even if	Zelfs als
Afterwards	Na, achteraf, nadien
Worse	Slechter
Where	Waar
Everything	Alles
Somewhere	Ergens
What	Wat
Almost	Bijna
There	Daar, er

Afterwards is worse
Achteraf is slechter
Even if I go now
Zelfs als ik nu ga
Where is everything?
Waar is alles?
Maybe somewhere
Misschien ergens
What? I am almost there
Wat? Ik ben er bijna
Where are you?
Waar ben je?
You and I
Jij en ik
Where is the airport?
Waar is het vliegveld?

*In the Dutch language, *daar* means "there," while *er* means "over there."
*In Dutch, "you" could either translate *je, jij, jou, u* (formal).
Je/jij is the nominative informal "you" (*u* is the formal), *je/jou* is the accusative
"you" (formal: *u*), and *je/jou* is the dative "you" (formal: *u*).
Nominative simply means "you." "You are Dutch?" / *Je/jij bent Nederlands?*
Accusative is the direct object: "I see you" / *ik zie je/jou* or "I love you" / *ik hou van je/jou.*
Dative is the indirect object in the sentence (from someone / to someone / for someone):
- "I must give you" / *ik moet je/jou geven*
- "I want to show you" / *ik wil je/jou laten zien*
Plural "you"
- nominative, accusative, and dative form is *jullie.*
The formal version of *u* is normally only used in formal organizations for people of a
higher rank and in daily conversations for people who are older than you. E.g. some
children will use the formal version for their grandparents; other children won't. But for
strangers, the formal version is used.
Where there are two options *(je/jij or je/jou),* these are interchangeable.

18

House / home	Huis / thuis
In / at	In / bij
Car	Auto
Already	Al
Good morning	Goedemorgen
How are you?	Hoe gaat het met je/jou?
Where are you from?	Waar kom je vandaan?
Me	Me / mij
Hello	Hallo
What is your name?	Wat is je/jouw naam?
How old are you?	Hoe oud ben je/jij?
Son	Zoon
Daughter	Dochter
Your	(form) Uw / (inf) jouw
Very	Erg
Hard	Moeilijk
Still	Nog, nog steeds
So (as in then)	Dus

She is without a car, so maybe she is still at the house?
Zij heeft geen auto, dus misschien is zij nog bij het huis?

I am already in the car with your son and daughter
Ik ben al in de auto met jouw zoon en dochter

Good morning, how are you today?
Goedemorgen, hoe gaat het met je vandaag?

Hello, what is your name?
Hallo, wat is je/jouw naam?

How old are you?
Hoe oud ben je/jij?

This is very hard, but it's not impossible
Dit is erg moeilijk, maar het is niet onmogelijk

Where are you from?
Waar kom je vandaan?

* "He is" is *hij is* / "she is" is *zij is;* however, in questions, the verb and subject change position; "she is?" *is zij?* / "he is?" *is hij?*

Waar ... vandaan means "from where." The word van has many meanings, one of which is "from," but it cannot be used like this (van) in this sentence. It is a fixed expression and you have to use *vandaan* in this case.

* *Zij heeft geen auto* = "She has no car." "She is without a car" cannot be mirror translated into Dutch.

*In Dutch, "your" – (formal) *Uw* / (informal) *jouw* – it is grammatically correct to use both, although Dutch people will have a strong preference for one of them depending on the sentence. This is something that cannot be explained; it is chosen based on a feeling.

Thank you/thanks	Dank je / bedankt
For	Voor
A	Een
This is	Dit is
Time	Tijd
But / however	Maar, echter
No / Not	Nee / niet
I am not	Ik ben niet
Away	Weg
That	Dat
Similar	Vergelijkbaar
Other / Another	Ander / andere
Side	Kant
Until	Tot, totdat
Yesterday	Gisteren
Without us	Zonder ons
Since	Sinds
Day	Dag
Before	Voor, voordat

Thanks for anything
Bedankt voor alles
It's almost time
Het is bijna tijd
I am not here, I am away
Ik ben niet hier, ik ben weg
That is a similar house
Dat is een vergelijkbaar huis
I am from the other side
Ik ben van de andere kant
But I was here until late yesterday
Maar ik was hier tot laat gisteren
Since the other day
Sinds de andere dag

I say / I am saying	Ik zeg
What time is it?	Wat is de tijd? / hoe laat is het?
I want	Ik wil
Without you	Zonder jou
Everywhere /wherever	Overal / waar dan ook
I go / I am going	Ik ga
With	Met
My	Mijn
Cousin	(Male) Neef, (Female) Nicht
I need / I must	Ik heb … nodig / Ik moet
Right now	Direct, nu
Night	Nacht
To see	Zien
Light	Licht
Outside	Buiten
That is	Dat is
To be	Zijn
I see / I am seeing	Ik zie

I am saying no / I say no
Ik zeg nee
I want to see this during the day
Ik wil dit tijdens de dag zien
I see this everywhere
Ik zie dit overal
I am happy without my cousins here
Ik ben blij zonder mijn (M)neven/(F)nichten hier
I need to be there at night
Ik moet daar 's nachts zijn
I see light outside
Ik zie licht buiten
What time is it right now?
Hoe laat is het nu? / Wat is de tijd nu?

*A very important rule in Dutch: whenever a conjugated verb is the first part of the sentence, it stays the same as its English counterpart. But in case the conjugated verb isn't the first part of the sentence, it will usually be placed at the end: "because I want this car" / *omdat ik deze auto wil*. Whenever a sentence contains two verbs, the second verb will usually appear at the end of the sentence (unlike in English in which the infinitive always follows the conjugated verb): "I want to see this in the day" / *Ik wil dit overdag zien*. There are exceptions, though. For example, the verb "to know" / *weten* isn't moved to the end of the sentence in this case: "I must know where is the house" / *Ik moet weten waar het huis is*.

*In Dutch, *'s* is a fixed expression
"At night" – *'s nachts* / "In the morning" – *'s morgens* /"In the afternoon" – *'s middags*.
*This *isn't* a phrase book! The purpose of this book is solely to provide you with the tools to create *your own* sentences!

Place	Plaats
Easy	Makkelijk
To find	Vinden
To look for/to search	Zoeken
Near / Close	Dichtbij
To wait	Wachten
To sell	Verkopen
To use	Gebruiken
To know	Weten
To decide	Beslissen
Between	Tussen
Two	Twee
To	Te, naar
Next to	Naast
That *(conjunction)*	Dat

This place is easy to find
Deze plaats is makkelijk te vinden
I need to look for you next to the car
Ik moet zoeken naar jou naast de auto
I am saying to wait until tomorrow
Ik zeg te wachten tot morgen
It's easy to sell this table
Het is makkelijk om deze tafel te verkopen
I want to use this
Ik wil dit gebruiken
I must know where is the house
Ik moet weten waar het huis is
I must decide between both places
Ik moet beslissen tussen beide plaatsen
I need to know that everything is ok
Ik moet weten dat alles oké is

*In Dutch, the article "this" preceding a noun is *dit, deze. Deze*is masculine
nominative, feminine nominative is *deze*, and neutral nominative is *dit*.
*In Dutch, there are two forms for expressing "to," *naar* and *te. Naar* is "to" when
talking about going to a specific place. E.g. "I am going to New York/the library/
home." In combination with verbs, it is *te*.
*"I need" / *ik heb nodig* and "I must" / *Ik moet* is used interchangeably throughout this
program when translating "I need."

Because	Omdat
To buy	Kopen
Both	Beide / allebei
Them / they / their	Hen / zij / hun
Each / Every	Elk, elke, ieder, iedere
Book	Boek
Mine	Mijn
To understand	Begrijpen
Problem / Problems	Probleem / problemen
I do / I am doing	Ik doe
Of	Van, over
To look	Kijken
Myself	Mezelf
Enough	Genoeg
Food	Eten, voedsel
Water	Water
Hotel	Hotel

I like this hotel because I want to look at the beach
Ik vind dit hotel leuk, omdat ik naar het strand wil kijken
I want to buy a bottle of water
Ik wil een fles water kopen
I do it like this each day
Ik doe het elke dag zoals dit
Both of them have enough food
Allebei hebben ze genoeg voedsel
That is the book, and that book is mine
Dat is het boek en dat boek is van mij
I need to understand the problem
Ik moet het problem begrijpen
From the hotel I have a view of the city
Van het hotel heb ik uitzicht over de stad
I can work today
Ik kan vandaag werken
I do my homework
Ik doe mijn huiswerk

*The Dutch grammatical rule concerning moving the second and third verb(s) to the end applies in most sentences unless the sentence is broken in parts, separated either by a comma or an "and."

I like	Ik vind ... leuk
There is	Daar is, Er is
There are	Daar zijn, Er zijn
Family / Parents	Familie / Ouders
Why	Waarom
To say	Zeggen
Something	Iets
To go	Gaan
Ready	Klaas
Soon	Snel, bijna
To work	Werken
Who	Wie
Important	Belangrijk, belangrijks

I like to be at home with my parents
Ik vind het leuk thuis te zijn met mijn ouders
I want to know why I have to say something important
Ik wil weten waarom ik iets belangrijks moet zeggen
I am there with him
Ik ben daar met hem
I am busy, but I need to be ready soon
Ik ben druk, maar ik moet bijna klaar zijn
I like to work
Ik vind het leuk te werken
Who is there?
Wie is daar?
I want to know if they are here, because I want to go outside
Ik wil weten of zij hier zijn, omdat ik naar buiten wil gaan
There are seven dolls
Er zijn zeven poppen

*In Dutch, if three verbs exist in the same sentence (Verb A, B, and C), Verb A is placed at the beginning of the sentence (as its English counterpart), while Verbs B and C are placed at the end and are inverted. So the chronological order is A, C, B. Take a look at the second sentence of this page (keep in mind that "to know" / weten is an exception).
*There is no verb for "like," so you have to translate it as "I find nice." You always have to put the object you like in between *vind* and *leuk*.

How much	Hoeveel
To take	Nemen
With me	Met mij
Instead	In plaats van
Only	Alleen
When	Wanneer
I can / can I?	Ik kan / Kan ik?
Or	Of
Were	Waren
Without me	Zonder mij
Fast	Snel
Slow	Langzaam
Cold	Koud
Inside	Binnen
To eat	Eten
Hot	Heet
To Drive	Rijden

How much money do I need to take?
Hoeveel geld moet ik meenemen?
Instead of this cake, I like that cake
In plaats van deze taart, vind ik die taart leuk
Only when you can
Alleen wanneer jij kan
They were without me yesterday
Zij waren zonder mij gisteren
I need to drive the car very fast or very slowly
Ik moet doe auto erg snel of erg langzaam rijden
It is cold in the library
Het is koud in de bibliotheek
Yes, I like to eat this hot for my lunch
Ja, ik vind het leuk dit warm te eten voor mijn lunch

*In Dutch, whenever asking a question, the pronoun follows the conjugated verb. As you can see in the first sentence: "how much money do I need to take?" / *Hoeveel geld moet ik meenemen?* The pronoun *ik* / "I" follows the conjugated verb *moet* / "I need."

To answer	Antwoorden
To fly	Vliegen
Today	Vandaag
To travel	Reizen
To learn	Leren
How	Hoe
To swim	Zwemmen
To practice	Oefenen
To play	Spelen
To leave	Verlaten
Many/much/a lot	Veel
I go to	Ik ga naar
First	Eerst / eerste
Time / Times	Tijd / Tijden

I need to answer many questions
Ik moet veel vragen beantwoorden
I want to fly today
Ik wil vandaag vliegen
I need to learn to swim
Ik moet leren zwemmen
I want to know everything about how to play better tennis
Ik wil alles weten over hoe beter tennis te spelen
I want to leave this here for you, when I go to travel the world
Ik wil dit hier laten voor jou, wanneer ik in de wereld ga reizen
Since the first time
Sinds de eerste tijd
The children are yours
De kinderen zijn van jou

*In Dutch, *uw* is the formal and *jouw* is the informal; however, "yours" is *jou*. *Dit zijn jouw kinderen* = "These are your children," however, *de kinderen zijn van jou* = "The children are yours."
*With the knowledge you've gained so far, now try to create your own sentences!

Nobody / Anyone	Niemand, iedereen
Against	Tegen
Us	Ons
To visit	Bezoeken
Mom / Mother	Mama/ Moeder
To give	Geven
Which	Welk, welke
To meet	Ontmoeten
Someone	Iemand
Just	Net
To walk	Wandelen
Around	Rond
Towards	Tegen
Than	Dan
Nothing	Niets

Something is better than nothing
Iets is beter dan niets
I am against him
Ik ben tegen hem
We go each week to visit my family
We gaan elke week mijn familie bezoeken
I need to give you something
Ik moet je iets geven
Do you want to meet someone?
Wil je iemand ontmoeten?
I am here also on Wednesdays
Ik ben hier ook op woensdagen
You do this everyday?
Je doet dit elke dag?
You need to walk around the house
Je moet rond het huis wandelen

I have	Ik heb
Don't	Niet
Friend	Vriend
To borrow	Lenen
To look like	Eruit zien als
Grandfather	Opa, grootvader
To want	Willen
To stay	Blijven
To continue	Verder gaan
Way	Weg
That's why	Daarom
To show	Laten zien
To prepare	Voorbereiden
I am not going	Ik ga niet

Do you want to look like Arnold?
Wil je eruit zien als Arnold?
I want to borrow this book for my grandfather
Ik wil dit boek lenen voor mijn opa
I want to drive and to continue on this way to my house
Ik wil rijden en verder gaan op deze weg naar mijn huis
I have a friend, that's why I want to stay in Utrecht
Ik heb een vriend, dat is waarom ik in Utrecht wil blijven
I don't want to see anyone here
Ik wil hier niemand zien
I need to show you how to prepare breakfast
Ik moet/wil je laten zien hoe ontbijt te maken
Why don't you have the book?
Waarom heb je het boek niet?
That is incorrect, I don't need the car today
Dat klopt niet, ik heb de auto niet nodig vandaag

*In Dutch, you would say "to **make** breakfast" and not "to prepare breakfast."

To remember	Onthouden
Dutch	Nederlands
Number	Nummer
Hour	Uur
Dark / darkness	Donker / Duisternis
About	Over, ongeveer
Grandmother	Oma, grootmoeder
Five	Vijf
Minute / Minutes	Minuut / minuten
More	Meer
To think	Denken
To do	Doen
To come	Komen
To hear	Horen
Last	Laatst, laatste

I need to remember your number

Ik moet je/jouw nummer onthouden

This is the last hour of darkness

Dit is het laatste uur duisternis

I want to come and to hear my grandmother speak Dutch today

Ik wil komen en mijn oma Nederlands horen praten vandaag

I need to think more about this, and what to do

Ik moet hier meer over denken en over wat te doen

From here to there, it's only five minutes

Van hier naar daar is het maar vijf minuten

To leave	Weggaan
Again	Nog een keer, nogmaals
The Netherlands	Nederland
To bring	Brengen
To try	Proberen
To rent	Huren
Without her	Zonder haar
We are	We zijn
To turn off	Uitzetten
To ask	Vragen
To stop	Stoppen
Permission	Toestemming

He needs to leave and rent a house at the beach
Hij moet weggaan en een huis bij het strand huren
We are here for a long time
We zijn hier voor lange tijd
I need to turn off the lights early tonight
Ik moet het licht vroeg uitdoen vandaag
We want to stop here
We willen hier stoppen
We are from Groningen
We komen uit Groningen
The same building
Hetzelfde gebouw
I want to ask for permission to leave
Ik wil vragen om toestemming om te vertrekken

*In Dutch, *Om* is a part of fixed expressions.
- "Ask for permission" = *vragen om toestemming*
- "Permission to" = *toestemming om te*

To open	Openen
To buy	Kopen
To pay	Betalen
Last	Laatst, laatste
Without	Zonder
Sister	Zus
To hope	Hopen
To live	Wonen, leven
Nice to meet you	Leuk je te leren kennen
Name	Voornaam
Last name	Achternaam
To return	Terugkomen
Enough	Genoeg
Door	Deur
On	Op
Our	Ons

I need to open the door for my sister

Ik moet de deur openen voor mijn zus

I need to buy something

Ik moet iets kopen

I want to get to know your sisters

Ik wil je zussen leren kennen

Nice to meet you, what is your name and your last name?

Leuk je te leren kennen, wat je is voornaam en je achternaam?

To hope for the better in the future

Op het beste hopen in de toekomst

I want to return from the United States and to live without problems in the Netherlands

Ik wil uit de Verenigde Staten terugkomen en zonder problemen leven in Nederland

Why are you sad right now?

Waarom ben je verdrietig nu?

Our house is on the mountain

Ons huis is op de heuvel

*In Dutch, "your" is *jouw*, however, in the case on this page, *je* is not the subject of the sentence, but the possessive determiner. In this sentence, it is interchangeable with *jouw*.

*In Dutch, *op* is a fixed expression: "To hope for" = *Hopen op*.

*This isn't a phrase book! The purpose of this book is solely to provide you with the tools to create your own sentences!

To happen	Gebeuren
To order	Bestellen
To drink	Drinken
Excuse me	Excuseer mij
Child	Kind
Woman	Vrouw
To begin / To start	Beginnen
To finish	Eindigen
To help	Helpen
To smoke	Roken
To love	Houden van
To talk / To Speak	Zu sprechen

This must happen today
Dit moet gebeuren vandaag
Excuse me, my child is here as well
Excuseer mij, mijn kind is hier ook
I love you
Ik hou van je/jou
I see you
Ik zie je/jou
I need you
Ik heb je/jou nodig
I want to help
Ik wil helpen
I don't want to smoke again
Ik wil niet weer roken
I want to learn to speak Dutch
Ik wil Nederlands leren spreken

*"I don't want" is *ik wil niet.*

To read	Lezen
To write	Schrijven
To choose	Kiezen
To teach	Leren, les geven
To close	Sluiten
To turn on	Aanzetten
To prefer	Verkiezen
To put	Neerleggen
Less	Minder
Sun	Zon
Month	Maand
I Talk	Ik spreek
Exact	Precies, exact(e)

I need this book, in order to learn how to read and write in Dutch because I want to teach in the Netherlands

Ik heb dit boek nodig, om te leren lezen en schrijven in het Nederlands omdat ik les wil geven in Nederland

I want to close the door of the house and not to turn on the light

Ik wil de deur van het huis dicht doen en het licht niet aan doen

I prefer to put the gift here

Ik verkies het cadeau hier neer te leggen

I want to pay less than you for the dinner

Ik wil minder dan jou betalen voor het diner

I speak with the boy and the girl in German

Ik spreek met de jongen en het meisje in het Duits

I see the sun today

Ik zie de zon vandaag

Is it possible to know the exact date?

Is het mogelijk de exacte datum te weten

To exchange	Ruilen, wisselen
To call	Bellen
Brother	Broer
Dad	Vader
To sit	Zitten
Together	Samen
To change	Veranderen
Of course	Natuurlijk
Welcome	Welkom
During	Tijdens
Years	Jaren
Sky	Hemel
Up	Boven
Down	Onder
Sorry	Sorry
To follow	Volgen
Her /hers	Haar
Big	**Groot**
New	Nieuw
Never	Nooit
His	Zijn

I never want to exchange this money at the bank
Ik wil dit geld nooit wisselen bij de bank
I want to call my brother and my dad today
Ik wil mijn broer en mijn vader bellen vandaag
Of course I can come to the theater, and I want to sit together with you and with your sister
Natuurlijk kan ik naar het theater komen en ik wil samen met jou en je zus zitten
I need to go down in order to see your new house
Ik moet naar beneden gaan om je nieuwe huis te zien
I can see the sky from the window
Ik kan de hemel van het raam zien
I am sorry, however he wants to follow her to the store
Het spijt me, echter wil hij haar naar de winkel volgen

*With the knowledge you've gained so far, now try to create your own sentences!

To allow	Zu Lassen
To believe	Zu glauben
Morning	Morgen
Except	Außer
To promise	Zu versprechen
Good night	Gute Nacht
To recognize	Zu erkennen
People	Leute
To move	Zu bewegen, umziehen
Far	Weit
Different	Verschieden, anderer
Man	Mann
To enter	Eintreten
To receive	Zu empfangen
Throughout	Durch und durch
Tonight	Heute Nacht
Through	Durch
Him	Hem

I need to allow him to go with us, he is a different man now

Ik moet hem toestaan met ons mee te gaan, hij is een andere man nu

I believe everything except for this

Ik geloof alles behalve dit

They need to recognize the people from the Netherlands very quickly

Zij moeten de mensen uit Nederland erg snel herkennen

I need to put your cat to another chair

Ik moet je kat op een andere stoel leggen

I see the sun in the morning from the kitchen

Ik zie de zon in de ochtend vanuit de keuken

I want his car

Ik wil zijn auto

To wish	Wensen
Bad	Slecht
To Get	Krijgen
To forget	Vergeten
Everybody / Everyone	Iedereenr
Although	Hoewel
To feel	Voelen
Great	Groot
Next	Volgende
To like	Leuk vinden
In front	Voor
Person	Persoon
Behind	Achter
Well	Goed
Goodbye	Tot ziens
Restaurant	Restaurant
Bathroom	Toilet
To sleep	Slapen

I don't want to wish anything bad
Ik wil je niet iets slechts wensen
I must forget everybody from my past
Ik moet iedereen van mijn verleden vergeten
I am close to the person behind you
Ik ben dichtbij de persoon achter jou
There is a great person in front of me
Er is een groot persoon voor mij
I say goodbye to my friends
Ik zeg tot ziens tegen mijn vrienden
In which part of the restaurant is the bathroom?
In welk deel van het restaurant is het toilet?
I want a car before the next year
Ik wil een auto voor het volgende jaar
I want to like the house, however it is very small
Ik wil dit huis leuk vinden, echter het is erg klein
I must go to sleep
Ik moet gaan slapen

To remove	Verwijderen
Please	Alsjeblieft
Beautiful	Mooi
To lift	Optillen
Include / Including	Inclusief
Belong	Behoren tot, horen
To hold	Houden
To check	Nakijken
Small	Klein
Real	Echt
Week	Week
Size	Maat, grootte
Even though	Hoewel
Doesn't	Niet
So	Erg *(very)* / dus *(then)*
Price	Prijs

She wants to remove this door, please
Zij wil deze deur verwijderen, alsjeblieft
This doesn't belong here, I need to check again
Dit hoort hier niet, ik moet het opnieuw nakijken
This week the weather was very beautiful
Deze week was het weer erg mooi
I need to know which is the real diamond
Ik moet weten welke de echte diamant is
We need to check the size of the house
We moeten de grootte van het huis nakijken
I want to lift this, so you need to hold it high
Ik wil dit optillen, dus je moet het hoog houden
I can pay this although the price is expensive
Ik kan dit betalen hoewel de prijs duur is
Including everything is this price correct?
Inclusief alles is deze prijs correct?

*In the sentence, "This week the weather was very beautiful" / *Deze week was het weer erg mooi,* "was"/*was* is the verb. So, this is the same as many of the earlier sentences.

BUILDING BRIDGES

In Building Bridges, we take six conjugated verbs that have been selected after studies I have conducted for several months in order to determine which verbs are most commonly conjugated, and which are then automatically followed by an infinitive verb. For example, once you know how to say, "I need," "I want," "I can," and "I like," you will be able to connect words and say almost anything you want more correctly and understandably. The following three pages contain these six conjugated verbs in first, second, third, fourth, and fifth person, as well as some sample sentences. Please master the entire program up until *here* prior to venturing onto this section.

I want	Ik wil
I need	Ik moet, Ik heb … nodig
I can	Ik kan
I like	Ik vind … leuk
I go	Ik ga
I have	Ik heb
I must	Ik moet

I want to go to my apartment
Ik wil naar mijn appartement gaan
I can go with you to the bus station
Ik kan met jou naar het busstation gaan
I need to walk to the museum
Ik moet naar het museum wandelen
I like to take the train
Ik vind het leuk om de trein te nemen
I am going to teach a class
Ik ga een klas les geven
I have to speak to my teacher
Ik moet met mijn leraar spreken

Please master pages #16-#38, prior to attempting the following pages!!

You want / do you want? - Je wil / wil je?
He wants / does he want? - Hij wil / wil hij?
She wants / does she want? - Zij wil / wil zij?
We want / do we want? - We willen / willen we?
They want / do they want? - Zij willen / willen zij?
You (plural) want - Jullie willen / willen jullie?

You need / do you need? - Je hebt nodig / heb je nodig?
He needs / does he need? - Hij heeft nodig / heeft hij nodig?
She needs / does she need? - Zij heeft nodig / Heeft zij nodig?
We need / do we need? - We willen / willen we?
They need / do they need? - Zij hebben nodig / Hebben zij nodig?
You (plural) need - Jullie hebben nodig / hebben jullie nodig?

You can / can you? - Je kan / Kan je?
He can / can he? - Hij kan / kan hij?
She can / can she? - Zij kan / kan zij?
We can / can we? - We kunnen / kunnen we?
They can / can they? - Zij kunnen / kunnen zij?
You (plural) can - Jullie kunnen / kunnen jullie?

You like / do you like? - Je vindt leuk? / vind je leuk?
He likes / does he like? - Hij vindt leuk / vindt hij leuk?
She like / does she like? - Zij vindt leuk / vindt zij leuk?
We like / do we like? - We vinden leuk / vinden we leuk?
They like / do they like? - Zij vinden leuk / vinden zij leuk?
You (plural) like - Jullie vinden leuk / vinden jullie leuk?

You go / do you go? -Je gaat / ga je?
He goes / does he go? - Hij gaat / gaat hij?
She goes / does she go? - Zij gaat / gaat zij?
We go / do we go? - We gaan / gaan we?
They go / do they go? - Zij gaan / gaan zij?
You (plural) go - Jullie gaan / gaan jullie?

You have / do you have? - Je hebt / heb je?
He has / does he have? - Hij heeft / heeft hij?
She has / does she have? - Zij heeft / heeft zij?
We have / do we have? - We hebben / hebben we?
They have / do they have? - Zij hebben / hebben zij?
You (plural) have - Jullie hebben / hebben jullie?

Please master pages #16-#38,
prior to attempting this page!

Do you want to go?
Wil je gaan?
Does he want to fly?
Wil hij vliegen?
We want to swim
We willen zwemmen
Do they want to run?
Willen zij rennen?
Do you need to clean?
Moet je schoonmaken?
Moeten jullie schoonmaken?
She needs to sing a song
Zij moet een liedje zingen
We need to travel
We moeten reizen
They don't need to fight
Zij moeten niet vechten
You (plural) need to see the film
Jullie moeten de film zien
Can you hear me?
Kan je me horen?
He can dance very well
Hij kan erg goed dansen
We can go out tonight
We kunnen vanavond uitgaan
They can break the wood
Zij kunnen het hout breken
Do you like to eat here?
Vind je het leuk om hier te eten?

He likes to spend time here
Hij vindt het leuk om hier tijd door te brengen
We like to fix the house
We vinden het leuk om het huis te repareren
They like to cook
Zij vinden het leuk om te koken
You (plural) like my house
Jullie vinden mijn huis leuk
Do you go to school today?
Ga je vandaag naar school?
He goes fishing
Hij gaat vissen
We are going to relax
Wij gaan uitrusten
They go to watch a film
Zij gaan een film kijken
Do you have money?
Heb je geld?
She must look outside
Zij moet naar buiten kijken
We have to sign our names
We moeten onze namen tekenen
They have to send the letter
Zij moeten de brief sturen
You (plural) have to order
Jullie moeten bestellen

Days of the Week

Sunday	Zondag
Monday	Maandag
Tuesday	Dinsdag
Wednesday	Woensdag
Thursday	Donderdag
Friday	Vrijdag
Saturday	Zaterdag

Seasons

Spring	Lente/voorjaar
Summer	Zomer
Autumn	Herfst
Winter	Winter

Cardinal Directions

North	Noord
South	Zuid
East	Oost
West	West

Colors

Black	Zwart
White	Wit
Gray	Grijs
Red	Rood
Blue	Blauw
Yellow	Geel
Green	Groen
Orange	Oranje
Purple	Paars
Brown	Bruin

Numbers

One	Één
Two	Twee
Three	Drie
Four	Vier
Five	Vijf
Six	Zes
Seven	Zeven
Eight	Acht
Nine	Negen
Ten	Tien

*"One" - *Één* - usually no accent on the capital, but when used in lower case, two accents: *één*.

CONGRATULATIONS, NOW YOU ARE ON YOUR OWN!

If you merely absorb the required three hundred and fifty words in this book, you will then have acquired the basis to become conversational in Dutch! After memorizing these three hundred and fifty words, this conversational foundational basis that you have just gained will trigger your ability to make improvements in conversational fluency at an amazing speed! However, in order to engage in quick and easy conversational communication, you need a special type of basics, and this book will provide you with just that.

Unlike the foreign language learning systems presently used in schools and universities, along with books and programs that are available on the market today, that focus on *everything* but being conversational, *this* method's sole focus is on becoming conversational in Dutch as well as any other language. Once you have successfully mastered the required words in this book, there are two techniques that if combined with these essential words, can further enhance your skills and will result in you improving your proficiency tenfold. *However*, these two techniques will only succeed *if* you have completely and successfully absorbed the three hundred and fifty words. *After* you establish the basis for fluent communications by memorizing these words, you can enhance your conversational abilities even more if you use the following two techniques.

The first step is to attend a Dutch language class that will enable you to sharpen your grammar. You will gain additional vocabulary and learn past and present tenses, and if you apply these skills that you learn in the class, together with the three hundred and fifty words that you have previously memorized, you will be improving your conversational skills tenfold. You will notice that, conversationally, you will succeed at a much higher rate than any of your classmates. A simple second technique is to choose Dutch subtitles while watching a movie. If you have successfully mastered and grasped these three hundred and fifty words, then the combination of the two—those words along with the subtitles —will aid you considerably in putting all the grammar into perspective, and again, conversationally, you will improve tenfold.

Once you have established a basis of quick and easy conversation in Dutch with those words that you just attained, every additional word or grammar rule you pick up from there on will be gravy. And these additional words or grammar rules can be combined with the three hundred and fifty words, enriching your conversational abilities even more. Basically, after the research and studies I've conducted with my method over the years, I came to the conclusion that in order to become conversational, you first must learn the words and then learn the grammar.

The Dutch language is compatible with the mirror translation technique. Likewise, with this language, you can use this mirror translation technique in order to become conversational, enabling you to communicate even more effortlessly. Mirror translation is the method of translating a phrase or sentence, word for word from English to Dutch, by using these imperative words that you have acquired through this program (such as the sentences I used in this book. Latin languages, Middle Eastern languages, and Slavic languages, along with a few others, are also compatible with the mirror translation technique. Though you won't be speaking perfectly proper and precise Dutch, you will still be fully understood and, conversation-wise, be able to get by just fine.

CONCLUSION

Congratulations! You have completed all the tools needed to master the Dutch language, and I hope that this has been a valuable learning experience. Now you have sufficient communication skills to be confident enough to embark on a visit to The Netherlands, impress your friends, and boost your resume so good luck.

This program is available in other languages as well, and it is my fervent hope that my language learning programs will be used for good, enabling people from all corners of the globe and from all cultures and religions to be able to communicate harmoniously. After memorizing the required three hundred and fifty words, please perform a daily five-minute exercise by creating sentences in your head using these words. This simple exercise will help you grasp conversational communications even more effectively. Also, once you memorize the vocabulary on each page, follow it by using a notecard to cover the words you have just memorized and test yourself and follow that by going back and using this same notecard technique on the pages you studied during the previous days. This repetition technique will assist you in mastering these words in order to provide you with the tools to create your own sentences.

Every day, use this notecard technique on the words that you have just studied.

Everything in life has a catch. The catch here is just consistency. If you just open the book, and after the first few pages of studying the program, you put it down, then you will not gain anything. However, if you consistently dedicate a half hour daily to studying, as well as reviewing what you have learned from previous days, then you will quickly realize why this method is the most effective technique ever created to become conversational in a foreign language. My technique works! For anyone who doubts this technique, all I can say is that it has worked for me and hundreds of others.

Note from the Author

Thank you for your interest in my work. I encourage you to share your overall experience of this book by posting a review. Your review can make a difference! Please feel free to describe how you benefited from my method or provide creative feedback on how I can improve this program. I am constantly seeking ways to enhance the quality of this product, based on personal testimonials and suggestions from individuals like you.

Thanks and best of luck,

Yatir Nitzany

Made in the USA
Columbia, SC
15 July 2021